I0530614

JACQUELINE PIRTLE

COOL KIDS
WITH
COOL WITS

Dive into the belly of your truth

praise for jacqueline

"I love Jacqueline's books. They are great for adults and kids. We all have an inner genie and Jacqueline is teaching us how to hold on to it."

— Longtime Client and Reader

"Jacqueline's books are magickal teaching kids and adults how to listen to their intuition, emotions, and feelings."

— Longtime Client and Reader

"I love that Jacqueline Pirtle has written books about intuition that encourages youngsters and adults to listen to their inner voice and be who they came to be. I also love that she encourages parents to respect and allow their children to follow their inner genie, honor their auras when making decisions, and help them realize that they possess infinite wisdom and can learn how to tap into it. This is vital to a child's growth and development, yet I've never seen children books with these subject matters before. So, for that, I give Pirtle big kudos."

— Longtime Client and Reader

Copyright © 2024 Jacqueline Pirtle
www.FreakyHealer.com

All rights reserved. No part of this book may be reproduced or transmitted in any form or by any means, electronic or mechanical, including photocopying, recording, or by any information storage and retrieval system without the written permission of the publisher, except where permitted by law.

ISBN-13: 978-1-955059-61-9

Publisher: Jacqueline Pirtle - Freaky Healer

Editor-in-chief: Zoe Pirtle

Book cover design by Kingwood Creations kingwoodcreations.com

Author photo courtesy of Lionel Madiou madious.com

I dedicate this journal to ALL children in the universe.

You make the world a better place and for that I thank you from the tips of my toes.

Dear parent and caregiver,

As a holistic practitioner, energetic living expert, and emotional intelligence teacher I have written over 16 books for adults and children supporting people to live a more conscious, mindful, and happier life.

You can find out more at:
FreakyHealer Store
www.freakyhealer.com

Hope you'll take a look!

Happiest,
Jacqueline

claim it!

This journal belongs to:

_____

_____

What's your happy place?
Go there, stay there, and never leave!

introduction

Hey cool kid with a cool wit,

What does it really mean to be a kid, or even more precisely to be yourself as a child, and have you ever heard of Energetic Profiling™?

I bet you have not and maybe don't even know how powerful you actually are, especially when you understand yourself and the world better.

Imagine that you are energy and that all your energy has information stored inside of it. You job is to sense that energy and translate what you sense into thoughts, then words, which create feelings to let you know how you feel—good or bad. Good feelings signal that you live according to your true reasons of why you are here on earth, as your physical body, whereas bad feelings mean that you are not aligned with yourself fully and completely.

This journal is your roadmap to figuring out your energy and discovering yourself to create your own Energetic Profile™.

By following the adventurous journey in this book you will dive straight into the belly of your truth, leading you to find out the deepest meaning of who you really are, why you are here, and what it all means to begin with.

Powerful stuff, I know!

So, kid, are you ready to take the leap and jump into your own magick to then maybe, possibly, and probably share your wisdom with other kids and adults?

I sure hope you say yes, because in some strange way I know that you have it in you to teach the whole wide world about living a happy and fun life.

Okay then detective, let's go and search for your clues!

And remember, you are a hero!

Your biggest fan and fellow detective,

Jacqueline

(All of the above counts for parents, grandparents, and caretakers of young people too!)

P.S. At the end of this journal you will find some extra pages in case you turn into a writing machine and don't have enough space for all your results and findings—and even your urges to doodle or draw.

Go fill them up and have a blast!

DAY 1

Imagine you are given 30 days to figure out who you are! Like a detective or spy, you must find out the deepest secrets about yourself, how you feel and think, but also learn about your superpowers, wishes and dreams, strengths, talents, and what you like or don't like.

For this quest you get to choose a special outfit and hat, your favorite vehicle (car, ship, rocket, dragon, bird, butterfly, fairy-wings...) to drive or fly wherever you need to go to investigate.

You also get to pack your own suitcase or bag with your favorite food, drinks, and everything you want to bring on this adventure leading you deep into the belly of your truth. Are you ready?

But before you take off tomorrow, write down your plan so you are the best prepared detective ever! What will you wear? Will you fly, drive, or walk—and on what? What's in your suitcase, or bag? Don't forget to make a food list!

_____

_____

_____

_____

_____

_____

_____

DAY 2

Today's the day, detective! Hope you are dressed with your suitcase or bag in hand, vehicle in place—so hop on, close your eyes for a minute, breathe, and let's go!

The first quest is your full name. You have one or even many, right? Write your full name on the line below.

_____

How do you like your name to be pronounced? Say it aloud, yell it if you must!

How do you feel about your name, or when you say your name? What does your name mean to you? If your name would have a color, what would it be? What superpowers do you think your name possesses? What magick is your name capable of?

Write about your investigative findings below:

_____

_____

_____

_____

_____

_____

_____

DAY 3

Bravo detective! Yesterday you investigated your name and got closer to your truth. Today and the next few days it's all about numbers, but don't worry we are not talking math here. Instead, we are tackling your birthday numbers and the special meaning they possess.

Do I have your attention? Are you dressed, your suitcase packed, ready to dive into this deep wisdom?

First, write down your full birthdate (day, month, year):

_____

Next, look at the number of your birthday only for a minute or so (tomorrow we will research the rest of your magickal numbers).

Then, close your eyes and think about that birthday number. What does your birthday number feel like for you? What special powers do you see, or feel, in that number? Is it a happy, funny, creative, or even smart number?

Lastly, open your eyes and write down your birthday number clues:

_____

_____

_____

_____

_____

DAY 4

Yesterday you filled yourself with the superpower of your birthday number. Today, you will dive into the adventure of your birth month - either the number or the word - because it's an important puzzle piece to who you really are.

To make sure you can focus with a razor-sharp detective mind, write down your birth month, pack your mental bag with what's needed for an amazing month like that, then read what you wrote for a while!

_____

Now close your eyes and take a deep breath. Think about your birth month. What do you see, feel, hear, and think about it? Is it a loud month or a quiet one, a small or big one, and how strong is it?

When ready, open your eyes and write down the traces of wisdom you have received from your birth month.

_____

_____

_____

_____

_____

_____

DAY 5

Hurray, detective! You already know so much more about yourself, but are you ready to go even bigger? Can you handle a huge number like your birth year—and open your eyes and ears gigantically to take in all that information about you?

You absolutely can, so say "Yes!" and grab whatever support you need out of your suitcase. Make sure your head is not too hot or cold while writing down your birth-year. Look at it piercingly!

_____

Now close your eyes, push out your loudest whistle and let all pieces of evidence your birth-year is giving you come in. Do you smell it, can you feel it, are you getting your big vision?

Quick, open your eyes and write down these important pointers of your big birth-year number. It's your big truth of who you are.

_____

_____

_____

_____

_____

_____

_____

DAY 6

Party, party! Pretend it's your birthday today and, with your eyes and mouth wide open, that you are looking at the biggest, bestest, most amazing cake you have ever seen. Tip: just roll with it, even if it's not your special day today!

What kind of cake are you looking at? What flavor is it, how big, what's the form and color? Most importantly, how many candles are on it—how old are you today? Write down your real age, as the number or word:

_____

_____

Now look at your age, take a deep belly-breath and fill your lungs with loads of magick and mystery. Then answer these questions: how do you like your age—what do you like about your age? How do you feel being this age? What color does your age represent? What energy does your age feel like? If your age could wear clothes, how would your age dress?

_____

_____

_____

_____

_____

DAY 7

Let's spill yet another number secret of yours!

What time were you born? Ask your parents if you don't know because these birth-time numbers have magickal information for you. Write them down:

_____

Okay, let's start with your hour first. Look at that number and close your eyes. How do you feel about this honorable hour, what special meaning does it have for you?

_____

_____

_____

Now, let's check out the clues of your birth-minutes. Look at your minutes and close your eyes. How do you feel about your minutes? What does this unique timing mean to you?

_____

_____

_____

_____

DAY 8

Detective, you are a time-traveler in possession of a special power called imagination! Today, and tomorrow, you have to use it to go back to when you were born; both days for different reasons and special investigations. Are you ready-set-go and packed for a couple days of babyhood?

Where you were born is no coincidence. You were meant to be born there, it's your place of wonders. Go ahead, time-traveler, list your special birthplace:

_____

Now close your eyes and feel yourself as a tiny newborn baby. How did it look when you were born, how did you feel, being so new and young? How did you like your birth-place? Do you get a special sense or remember something special about it?

_____

_____

_____

_____

_____

_____

_____

DAY 9

Lightbulb moment! You are energy, you are made of energy, and you are always speaking, breathing, and acting as energy. Everything about you is about energy—and your energy is always changing. How cool is that?!

So the first quest of today is to give the energy you are right now a descriptive word. What is it?

_____

Next, step into your time-traveler imagination-power again and go way back to the day you took your first breath. Are you there?

Now close your eyes and sense the energy of that first breath, because it holds the secret to your superpower you came into this life with. How does it feel? How does it look; what color would you give it? And what special superpower does your first-breath-energy have? Fun fact, you still are that superpower!

_____

_____

_____

_____

_____

_____

Woahhhh! Guess what, detective?

You have an inner genie inside your body—it's in your head, heart, stomach… it's everywhere, it's part of you, and it's invisible. You can't grab it, it's like air, and it's pure magick.

Today we investigate the part of your inner genie inside your head—we leave your heart, stomach, and more for the next few days.

Are you ready? Have you packed good thinking-food for your head—are you on your preferred travel machine? Then close your eyes.

Imagine taking the deepest trip into your head in the hopes to find your inner genie, showing itself as a voice, talking to you. Sometimes it's loud and other times it's little, then it's slow or really fast.

Ask this inner genie living in your head: "Can you hear me?" "What do you want to tell me?" "What do I need to know about myself?"

When you have your answers, open your eyes and write down your investigative results about what your inner voice told you.

_____

_____

_____

_____

_____

DAY 11

Today's adventure takes place in your heart, the super-power-engine that creates your love, joy, and happiness. To get a base-line, how big is your heart, love, joy, and happiness? Gigantic, huge, big, medium, small?

_____

_____

Time to travel! Imagine hopping into your favorite vehicle to go meet your inner genie in your heart. Be dressed and take a full suitcase, you never know what tools you need or how long this excursion will take. Almost forgot, pack a mental microscope! Now put your hands to your heart, feel your heart, then close your eyes and ask your inner genie: "What do I feel?" "How do I feel?" Write down what it tells you:

_____

_____

Next imagine looking at your heart through a microscope. What do you see—an engine capable of super-love, happiness, joy? What color do you see? Is your heart smiling at you?

_____

_____

_____

Detective, today's job requires your bravery because you are meeting eye to eye with your inner genie in your deep-dark stomach—the center of your knowing.

Have you ever picked out a special rock from a pile of many rocks knowing for sure that this one is the best rock for you—or grabbed a favorite sticker from a whole sticker booklet just because you knew that it's the one? Yes or no? What did that knowing feel like to you?

_____

_____

That knowing is your inner genie in your stomach!

Close your eyes and put your hands onto your belly, breathe and smile. Imagine yourself ready, prepared, and with bravery as your backbone flying with speed into your deep dark belly, where it's quiet, peaceful, but also a little spooky. Once arrived ask your stomach genie: "What do I know?" "What do I need to know?" "What do I want to know?"

Take note of your detective work:

_____

_____

_____

_____

Your lungs have a superpower! It's your breath, and like an invisible genie, every breath in fills the tanks of your lungs with magick while every breath out makes space for more magick by cleaning out all non-magick.

Go ahead, close your eyes and take a big breath, then let it go. How big are your lung-tanks—how much magick can they hold? How does filling up your tanks with magick feel?

_____

_____

Now, explorer, let's get you to where the story of the superpower of your lungs really started: back to your first breath. Yes, you have already sensed the energy of your first breath. Do you remember? If not go check Day 9, if yes, let's continue…

Close your eyes, pretend you are being born and are taking your very first breath on earth. Come on, breathe in, make it a big one!

How does this superpower of your lungs feel? Powerful, exciting, happy? How much magick did your lung-tanks fill up with? Do you think taking deep breaths now can fill you with the same magick than your first breath as a baby?

_____

_____

_____

Detective, you are also a wizard and you know it! So what are you waiting for, it's time to put on your wizard hat of answers to get to the bottom of your purest wisdom ever! But before we dig deep, how does your magician-tool fit on your head? How does it look—and how do you feel having such a wise hat?

_____

_____

Now take a deep breath and close your eyes while putting your lazer-sharp focus onto your wisdom-hat. Then ask it: What am I here to do on earth? What magick am I here to share? What is my job, besides being alive as an earthling?

_____

_____

_____

_____

_____

_____

_____

Okay detective, grab your most powerful coat and shoes, it's going to be a strong day because you are facing a powerful energy, one that can't be denied. Any idea what it could be?

_____

_____

You know that feeling when you love a hobby or activity so much that you would give or do anything for it? Or when you think you'll never make it forward in life if you don't get to do it ever again? You would even trade something favorite for it, or fight for it or against anyone standing in your path and power? Is that a yes or a no?

_____

That, most amazing adventurer, is your passion! What do you feel passionate about? When does your most powerful passion strike? And how do you feel when your passion is being denied?

_____

_____

_____

_____

_____

Detective, put on a thinker-shirt, squint your eyes real seriously and pinch your lips because it's going to be an interesting day today. You are getting to the bottom of the purpose of a bathtub!

You'll find out about the "why" later... For now just go with it!

Picture a bathtub and its impressive job of holding a lot of water, for you to jump in the tub, splash around like a whale, and then hop out squeaky clean and probably smiling like a puppy dog.

That's some powerful purpose that bathtub holds, don't you think?

Name one other thing that has such a potent purpose of helping you in your daily life:

_____

_____

Now think of yourself and what amazing purpose you have living as an earthling on this planet! What's your purpose? Who are you helping with your purpose? And how does your purpose make you feel?

_____

_____

_____

_____

Time to go incognito spy-being, a secret talent hunt is in order. So do whatever it takes to stay unrecognized—put on your most secret glasses, bundle up big time, wear long socks, but definitely put on a mustache and hat.

First, go find the talents of your family members, pets, and friends. Pick at least 2 beings and search - dig deep, go underground if you must - for their talents. What are you finding, what impresses you about them?

_____

_____

_____

Now secretly go and search for your own talents! If it helps, try looking through someone else's eyes at yourself. Find your talents that impress you about yourself and the ones that others see in you. List at least 5 of them! What are they, how do they make you feel, and what are you doing with them?

_____

_____

_____

_____

_____

Detective! Psst! Today we are digging into the depth of L-O-V-E. But don't say it aloud, it's a bit of a secret mission.

First we need to study the different ways of L-O-V-E a bit. There's L-O-V-E for your toys, playtime, video gaming, music, crafting, or running outside. Then there's the L-O-V-E for your parents, siblings, pets, family, and friends—or the L-O-V-E for doing nothing, sleeping, or pulling prank on someone.

However, we are on the quest for another L-O-V-E and it's the most powerful one ever! So grab a gigantic mental microscope, and a snack while at it, and let's get to the bottom of what you need to know about: Your L-O-V-E for yourself!

What does your L-O-V-E for yourself feel like? Describe it, so you know what to look for when searching under the giant microscope:

_____

_____

Then imagine putting your whole body under the huge microscope. Scan where this powerful L-O-V-E for yourself sits in your body. Can you find it in your head, heart, stomach? Are there traces in your legs, feet, arms, and hands?

_____

_____

_____

Hey escape specialist! It just so happens that a mighty blanket of feelings is coming for you. It's gigantic, about to wrap around you so tight you are unable to move, think, or do anything anymore.

That blanket of feelings has no bad intentions and is a normal part of you, but it's here to see if you can figure out a way to tame your feelings, unwrap yourself from its hold, and take control of all your millions of feelings that are making up your feelings-blanket.

Are you ready for this most sensible expedition? What does your blanket of feelings look like, what color is it, and how big are we talking here? What feelings are in that blanket? How will it wrap you up—fully or partially, vertically or horizontally? How do you feel all wrapped up in your feelings-blanket?

_____

_____

_____

Next, how will you unwrap yourself, what's your escape plan? How will you gain control of your feelings? What's your strategy to feel all your feelings while staying unwrapped? Plus, what are your favorite feelings?

_____

_____

_____

Every good detective has a thinking machine built into their smart heads. It is stronger than a mountain and can get things done faster than a fighter jet can fly. You are no different, you have the most powerful tool right in your head! Can you guess what it is?

_____

_____

Now imagine that there is a secret slide going into your brain, one that only you know about and is most fun to jump on and slide. The entrance is on top of your head and to open you have to tap the crown of your head three times. What are you waiting for? Tap, jump, and slide! Wheeeeee!!!

Upon arrival in your super-power thinking machine, your brain, what does it look like there, and how does it feel? Details please!

_____

_____

_____

_____

_____

_____

Trick question, detective! Do you know that your thinking machine, your brain, produces thoughts? And did you also know that your thoughts feed your mind? I am pretty certain you have a very strong and powerful mind, right? Yes or no?

_____

Then, smart one, how does your mind feel when you feed it positive thoughts—you know, the ones that feel good and come from your heart? What's your favorite thought of all time?

_____

_____

_____

_____

In comparison, how does your mind feel when you feed it negative or the not-good feeling thoughts?

_____

_____

_____

_____

DAY 22

Hey magician, imagine you just got your hands on a magick wish-dream wand! How did it come to you—did you get it in a heist, was it a gift, or did you find it on a bench in the park? What does it look like—what material is it made of, what color, and does it have writing on it? Most importantly, how do you use it and how does it activate your wishes and dreams?

_____

_____

_____

_____

_____

So you have the wand, but what are your wishes and dreams? The wand needs to know them so it can create and activate your deepest desires. Make your wishlist, detective!

_____

_____

_____

_____

_____

Hey super spy, imagine entering a wonderland filled with play, fun, toys, crafting, sports, playgrounds, and anything else that makes your heart sing—while pretending not be a detective hard at work.

What would your personal playground look like?

What makes you happy? What do you like to play? How crazy do you choose to get?

_____

_____

_____

_____

_____

_____

_____

_____

_____

_____

_____

_____

DAY 24

Every adventurer has to eat in order to get good work done and not get hangry. What is food for you? How do you feel about eating? How do you like to eat—what foods make you happy, and why?

_____

_____

_____

_____

_____

Food fact: food wants you to play with it - not fight - because having fun with food is part of being a successful hero. How do you like to play with your food - we're not talking about throwing it at walls - and what's the deep truth about you and food?

_____

_____

_____

_____

_____

Pack your bag adventurer, you are going on a winning trip, and since you don't really know what you will encounter make sure you pack for every possible scenario. Are you ready?

_____

_____

Now close your eyes and picture a winning situation; you being a winner, having a winner day, winning at whatever you are doing. You are a winner!

How do you feel? What are you doing, what is the winning experience you are having? Are you smiling? What are you wearing? Do you feel strong and bold? Are you happy? Who is with you?

_____

_____

_____

_____

_____

_____

_____

_____

DAY 26

Hey detective, let's do some fact checks over the next few days:

Fact 1:

What should the world know about you? What do you want your friends and family to know about you? What are you proud of yourself for?

_____

_____

_____

_____

_____

_____

_____

_____

_____

_____

_____

Fact 2:

Imagine you can do whatever you want to do. What will that be and how do you want to do it? Where will you do your favorite thing, and what will you need to do what you want to do?

_____

_____

_____

_____

_____

_____

_____

_____

_____

_____

_____

_____

_____

DAY 28

Fact 3:

You have a super power! What does your superpower look like? What color is it? Are you holding it, or is it inside of you? Is it big or small?

_____

_____

_____

_____

_____

_____

_____

_____

_____

_____

_____

Fact 4:

Imagine you could choose your perfect life. How would you like your life to be? Where would you want to live? What does it look like there?

_____

_____

_____

_____

_____

_____

_____

_____

_____

_____

_____

_____

Fact 5:

Imagine you get to give one gift (or more) to the world, to make it better and nicer. What would that be?

_____

_____

_____

_____

_____

_____

_____

_____

_____

_____

_____

_____

_____

bonus

Because hey, you don't want this search for your truth to end.

So keep on profiling detective, there's still so much to find out about yourself!

Find 15 words that describe you perfectly:

_____

_____

_____

_____

_____

_____

_____

_____

_____

_____

_____

_____

_____

_____

_____

DAY 32

List 15 foods that you love, love, love:

_____

_____

_____

_____

_____

_____

_____

_____

_____

_____

_____

_____

_____

_____

_____

_____

DAY 33

Name 15 activities that make you happy:

_____

_____

_____

_____

_____

_____

_____

_____

_____

_____

_____

_____

_____

_____

_____

Come up with 15 ways to be kind:

_____

_____

_____

_____

_____

_____

_____

_____

_____

_____

_____

_____

_____

_____

_____

_____

_____

What makes the world a better place? Think of 15 ideas:

_____

_____

_____

_____

_____

_____

_____

_____

_____

_____

_____

_____

_____

_____

_____

extra pages

How cool is it that you don't have to sweat the small stuff—like not having enough space for all your results and findings or to refrain the urge of doodling or drawing.

Just come on over here and use these extra pages for whatever needs you have to scratch, and most importantly, have fun while at it.

Cool Kids With Cool Wits

Cool Kids With Cool Wits

Cool Kids With Cool Wits

thank you!

Let's be honest here… I have a dream team!

I could not have finished this book without the help of talented, creative, and phenomenal professionals and the guidance of ALL children in my life.

From the bottom of my heart, I want to thank Zoe Pirtle for her editorial mastery; kingwoodcreations.com for their fun and polished book cover design; and madiouART.com for an amazing photo shoot.

I'd also like to extend a huge "Thank You!" to all fans of my work and books—I created this beautiful journal for ALL the young people in this universe.

Life is spectacular with kids on our side!

and last but not least

I truly hope your child - and you - enjoyed this journal as much as I loved writing it, and if that's so, it would be wonderful if you could take a short minute and leave a review on Amazon.com and Goodreads.com as soon as you can.

Your kind feedback helps other children and parents find my books more easily, and be happy faster. Consider it a happy deed for the children of the world. Thank you!

To find out more about my work and books check out:

www.freakyhealer.com

Jacqueline's Amazon Author Page

about the author

Jacqueline Pirtle is an internationally-renowned Mindful Happiness expert and the bestselling author of over 16 transformational personal growth books for adults and children.

She is a thought leader in the fields of mindfulness, happiness, energy work, energetic living and businessing, wholesome healing, and the teachings of one's soul.

Jacqueline has over 28 years of experience and has helped thousands of clients all over the world to discover their own happiness and how to live a conscious and mindfully aligned life filled with health, happiness, abundance, and success.

As the owner of *FreakyHealer* she has shared her solid teachings through her bestselling books, podcasts *The Weekly Freak & The Corporate Happiness Show*, sessions, workshops, courses and programs, talks and presentations with clients worldwide. She holds international degrees in holistic health and natural living and is certified in hypnosis for PTSD and a Reiki Master.

Her highly effective healing work has been featured in print and online magazines, podcasts, radio shows, on TV, and in the documentaries *The Overly Emotional Child* by *Learning Success*, available on *Amazon Prime* and Hacking Happiness.

www.ingramcontent.com/pod-product-compliance
Lightning Source LLC
Chambersburg PA
CBHW061324120626
46546CB00007B/2661